Yolanda McCutcheon

LIVE YOUR LIFE ON PURPOSE, NO EXCUSES

LIVE YOUR LIFE
ON PURPOSE,
NO EXCUSES

Yolanda McCutcheon

ISBN: 0692429433

ISBN-13: 978-0692429433

Dedication

This book is dedicated to my Grandmom Bessie Watlington. Grandmom I wish you could be here to see my dreams, and prayers come to fruition. I thank you so much for all the prayers you spoke over my life. I know you are enjoying Heaven, and making sure Angels are surrounding us down here at all times. I will never forget one of the last things you told me. "Never forget about God, and always keep him first". I will always remember and live by that rule, Grandmom. I love you and miss you dearly.

I would also like to dedicate this book to my mom Maxine, and my boys, Nameer & Quadeir.

Mom, thank you for always believing in me, and instilling in me the belief that I could be anything that I wanted to be. Thank you for loving me through those rough teenage years, and never giving up on me. I am so honored that God gave me such an amazing mom. I love you.

Nameer & Q, thank you for understanding Mommy's work schedule and all the sacrifices we went through to get to where we are in life. You guys have had to share, with me, the many women and men I help in my purpose. I love you even more for that. You guys are my why. You are what keeps me focused, dedicated and driven. I thank you and love you very much.

Contents

What People Are Saying About Yolanda

Yolanda is living proof that you should never allow your circumstances to dictate your future. Despite all odds, she has succeeded in life and business and has made it her mission to help others realize their full potential. Yolanda pushes you past your excuses and shows the possibilities. She is definitely someone to attach to.

Vicki Irvin, Superwoman Lifestyle
www.superwomanlifestyle.com

Yolanda is a tireless entrepreneur and is relentless in her pursuit of success. She truly understands the incredible dynamic that results from the infusion of passion into what you provide to the world via your business. Yolanda's perseverance is one of the things that I admire most about her. In a world full of inconsistencies and unreliable people it is refreshing to be able to rely on Yolanda being who I know her to be: dealmaker, planner, doer, visionary, and someone whose word means something!

Deon B. Browning, Esq., LL.M,
Browning Legal Group
www.BrowningLG.com

Yolanda is a visionary, energetic, compassionate, euphoric, spirited, inspirational, creative, and honest lady in a world filled with coal. Her desire, energy, and compassion to help others to become happy and successful in life without using them for economic or social gains, is rare today. I have watched her inspire, motivate, and change lives one person at a time. Her approach is simple, honest, realistic, straight from the heart, and personable. This makes her a priceless diamond in a world overflowing with cold, dishonest, insensitive, non-caring, and manipulative people. If you want the truth, inspiration, purpose, motivation, and you are willing to work hard for your happiness and success in life, this book is a must read especially for young ladies! You will be happy and successful when you find, pursue, and begin Living Your Life On Purpose!!!!

Coach Ike Williams

Yolanda has always been an entrepreneur. Even as a small child she knew how to make money. If she was not selling rice crispy treats, water ice or candy, she was doing hair, nails and body massages. This led her to network marketing. She finally found her purpose. She loves helping people and transforming lives. I am so proud of her accomplishments and can't wait to see what happens next. God bless you in all you do.

Love, Mom

Maxine Casidy, Maxi's Kids Child Care

The steps of a good women are ordered by the Lord. I've known Yolanda since she was 2 days old. Wow, is what I can say about what God has done in this young lady. A mother, an awesome mother, a daughter an awesome daughter, and I can even say even an awesome grand daughter, which I can say as her grandmother was my sister in the Lord.

I know I can look back and see how when Yolanda ran track she was motivated to be the best, the number 1, so that just showed me as she went through her life she always wanted to be the very very best. I'm just pleased to have her in my life and to know her so. When I think about her growing up right next door to me all these years, and seeing how God was developing such a young woman as she has become today to be so motivated to do and be all that God has planned for her.

I really believe she is walking in the destiny that God has already planned for her from the beginning, and I know this book is an encouragement to someone when they see what God has done in Yolanda's life, and he has no respective person and he can do the same thing in your life.

She is a excellent young lady, and I thank God for her all the time.

Dianne Jenkins

Live Your Life on Purpose, No Excuses

There are times when we all find an excuse that holds us back, or pushes us further away from our purpose. We all have dreams, goals and a purpose. Never let anyone or anything stop you from chasing your dreams, catching them and living your Life on Purpose, No Excuses.

The Beginning

As far back as I can remember, I was a kid that could sell anything. Anything I could get my hands on, I was selling it, from gemp jewelry down to Rice Crispy treats, even buying candy wholesale and selling it in school. In high school I was called "the candy girl."

Before my candy selling days, I loved to sing. I remember being in the school choir and the district choir. All my teachers and family just knew I would grow up to be a singer. I will never forget what my fourth grade teacher Miss Webster said, "One day when I am sitting back in my rocking chair I will see you gracing the stage singing your heart out." Just the thought of her believing in me still makes me smile to this day.

Well it wasn't long after my singing days that I became a track runner. I was pretty fast, beating most of the boys in a street race. I went on from middle school to run for a track club called Oaklane, where I met and built great lifelong friendships. In 9th grade I went to Overbrook High where I was a great asset to the team. What most people don't know is that I auditioned, and was accepted, to Creative And Performing Arts known as CAPA in Philly. My love for track and the encouragement from one of my Oaklane Coaches, Monique Leggette, convinced me I should go to Overbrook High.

My high school days painted life long memories. I always got pretty good grades, a little higher than average. I can tell you now, there was no experience like my high school experience. There were good days and then there were bad days. My ninth grade year I was all into my track career. I was pretty focused on something I loved to do. I remember practicing all the time, while others got to have fun. So I thought. I will never forget the day I asked my mom if I could quit track. My friends got to hang out after school, while I had to practice and compete. Well, the week before the Junior Olympics in the summer of 1996, I pulled my hamstring. I never experienced that type of pain before. I believe that was the beginning of the end of my running days. Even though I fully healed from that injury, my mind kept telling me I was hurt. I was afraid to run at full speed from then on. Since I was no longer running full time, I had a lot of time on my hands to get into other things. I always kept a job. I worked at McDonalds, CVS, ShopRite, and a telemarketing company. I was certainly no stranger to work. I loved the feeling of having my own money. I really didn't like to spend it, I like to let it accumulate, and I would find ways to increase it. I was really tight with my money, so I was pretty cautious about how I spent it.

It was around the 11th grade when I really stopped running and got more into a social crowd. I didn't realize that as soon as school let out for the day, everything could be so much fun. I was so used to either going right into practice or straight to work, that I didn't realize hanging out with my friends could be so great. For some strange reason we were called the "Barbie Dolls" in high school. We dressed to impress, and everyday just about felt like a fashion show. We were trendsetters. One day we all came to school wearing Dickie one piece jumpsuits. The next thing you know all the girls were doing it.

I guess I have to mention the days of all the fights. A lot of people say, "What?! You used to fight all the time?" Yeah, I kind of was a kid with a little temper, so I got into some fights. There was one time twenty-three girls came up to the school to fight us. Normally, there was always at least fifteen to twenty of us hanging out after school, but for some strange reason, on this day, there were only seven of us. The girls followed us, walking on the other side of the street until we got a couple blocks away from the school. Once we were off of school grounds they approached. What was supposed to be a one-on-one fight was a free for all. Let's just say the seven of us came out on top, and the other twenty-three found out what we were made of. Those were real times, and I'm glad I made it out without going to jail, or getting my face sliced. Sometimes that was the result of some of the fights. With all of that I did manage to maintain my grades. Outside of school, my friends and I would be everywhere; the plateau, concerts, Greek picnic, night clubs, South Street. If it was a hot spot we were there. I can say those days of being a teenager and growing up in West Philly was definitely a crazy, memorable and fun experience.

I remember thinking I was a grown up when I was a teenager. I had my own little money; I brought my own clothes, and even bought myself my first car. What I soon came to realize was the day that my life actually began, was when I was 18 years old and I found out that I was pregnant. It was a very, very difficult thing to tell anyone. I actually didn't tell my mom. I'll never forget the day that I found out. I was in my room, and I was holding a piece of paper. I went to the doctor's office that week, and they ran some tests and said, "You're pregnant." That was devastating. I was on schedule to go to college, and there were so many people depending on me to do well, to be successful, and I felt like I just let everybody down.

So I was in my room one day, and I had this pink piece of paper that had my results on it. I was trying to muster up the courage to go tell my mom that I was going to be a mother at 18 years old. I finally I got up enough courage (or so I thought) to tell my mom. I went into her room, and all I could do was just stand there and stare. I couldn't say anything. As much as I tried to get the words "I'm pregnant," out of my mouth, they just wouldn't come out.

My mom looked at me. I was staring at her, and all of a sudden tears just started pouring out of my eyes, rolling down my face. She looked and said, "What's the matter? What's wrong?" She was really concerned, and I couldn't say anything. She looked down at my hand and saw the pink piece of paper and asked, "What is this?" She took the paper from my hand, looked at it, and then looked at me, her eyes went back to the paper and she said, "You're pregnant?" She had this look of disappointment, hurt, and relief all at the same time, because she wasn't sure what was wrong with me. I remember she just hugged me, and kept telling me, "It's going to be alright. Everything is going to be alright."

To make matters worse, six months into my pregnancy, my son's father was sent to jail with a ten-year sentence. It was not only the devastation of letting people down, but also coming to the realization that I would have to raise this child on my own. That was the day I pretty much came into my own and said, "I'm not going to let this defeat me. I'm not going to let what other people think deter me or make me into who they think I am. I'm going to live the life that I am supposed to live, not only for me, but for my son." That is where it all started, and that is my beginning.

My situation was one that thousands and thousands of teenage girls go through. It is a point in life where you can decide to give up on your dreams, or make the best of your situation and run after what you want in life, no matter what. I had plans to finish college, but during my second semester at Penn State, I had to drop out to have my baby. In this situation it was not so much my dreams that I was worried about, it was the fact that I let down my parents and especially, my Grandmom. They tried to always instill so many values. "Do this, and don't do that." When I broke the rules and they find out about it, it really made it even worse. I think, "There's no way around this. There's no way of hiding it. It is what it is." The crazy thing about it is, that when they found out, they just had nothing but love; nothing but encouragement. "It's going to be okay, and life is not over. This is not the end. This is just a beginning. Now it's just going to be a little harder. You're going to have to work harder. You have someone else to take care of and not just yourself." That's the moment that I realized that I had to work double-time. It became more of a double effort for me.

I can tell you, I wanted everything to be okay, but there were many hard times. There were days I didn't think that I would make it. The reality of it all hit me one day like a ton of bricks. I thought I am going to be somebody's mom. I will be responsible for a person's life, feeding him clothing him, raising him to be an upstanding citizen. "Wow!" I thought. I worked at Wal-Mart and I sold Cutco knives. That still was not enough. I had to go on welfare. I will never ever forget that experience. Going into the welfare office was one of the worst experiences of my life. The people at this particular location, were rude and nasty. I sat in there for long periods of time, and then they wanted all of my personal information. All that for a couple hundred dollars!! It was a humiliating experience for me. I felt belittled. I made a vow to get off of welfare as soon as I could, even if I had to work two or three jobs.

In my darkest days of feeling like I couldn't do it, I reached deep down inside to all the moments my mom told me I could do anything I put my mind to. My desire to be somebody, and not be a hostage in that whole situation, helped me to push forward. I never thought that it would be easy, but at the same time, I realized that it's just something that I had to work through. It's another part of me, and it was going to make me stronger tomorrow than I was today.

Our beginnings and scars from life's experience are what make us who we are. Without life's challenges and experiences, we may not know what we are truly made of.

The Dream

I remember being a little girl who loved to sing. I had teachers and everybody would say, "I'm going to be sitting home in my rocking chair and see you on TV. You're going to be this fabulous, wonderful singer." My dream was something that started as a young kid. I didn't realize what it would be, but I always had this dream of a magnificent house; to the point where I actually drew the house out. To this day, I can still picture it.

I know that each and every one of us has a dream in us, and a lot of times you'll get people who try to deter that dream or try to crush it. I have four sisters, I sent one of my sisters, a text message, sharing with her this wonderful opportunity that I was introduced to. After I told her all the wonderful things about this opportunity, and she texted back and said, "What dreamer is this?" I will never, ever forget that day. Trying to crush my dreams. For a minute there, I started to think, "Am I a dreamer? Does anything I dream come true? Is that the same for everybody else?"

I started to doubt myself. Some people would think, "Dreams don't come true. Everybody dreams, but it's not the reality. So come back and snap into reality."

I just want to let everybody know that no matter what your dream is, everybody has a dream, and everybody has the ability to pursue that dream. Many of your dreams may be your purpose, it may be your goal, but it's your dream, and you don't want to let anybody take that away from you. You're allowed to dream. It's yours, so fight for that dream. Fight for your purpose, no matter what people say. And that's what I decided to do.

I decided to fight for my dream, and the day that I started to fight, I started to see it come to fruition. I started to see things happen when I started to just push and fight. Once I fought for it, literally, things started to fall into place.

Whatever you do, don't let anybody crush your dreams, because the dream-killers are real. You have to be careful with whom you actually share your dreams, because not everybody is prepared. Everybody is not able to see your dream. One thing my brother taught me a long time ago, is that everybody can't see the blueprint. Everybody can't read blueprints. They may be able to see the finished product, but there are only a select few who can actually see your dream as it's being built, so don't expect everyone to see or read blueprints until it's done.

As you can see, I've experienced the infamous dream-killers and dream-crushers for myself. When you have a dream and you're excited about it, you're passionate about it, and you share that with other people, you expect them to be just as excited for you as you are for yourself. The people you would least expect just don't appear to be all that happy about your decision to do more for yourself.

When dealing with dream-killers and dream-crushers, you have to be careful who you share your dreams with, because everybody is not prepared. You may get people cheerleading and saying, "Yes, yes! Go, team you!" But when you start to build that dream and people see it coming into fruition, they start to get jealous sometimes. You have to be very, very careful who you're sharing these dreams with. The way to go, in many cases, is don't bother opening up your mouth, because the moment you do the dream-crusher will be ready to get to work crushing your dreams. You don't want the negativity to deter you, so it's best to sometimes let people see the end results of your hard work and efforts. Don't let a dream-killer stop your process or your flow. Never let a dream-crusher crush your dreams. Your dream is your dream, it deserves to be seen in the world. Just look at the end result. Where are you trying to be? Where are you trying to go in life? And never stop until your dream has become your reality.

You never know, your dream or your purpose could help the next person. They may have seen the things that you're going through, even though people trying to pull you down or trying to deter your dreams. And when they see you have fought through it, that you've made it, that they too can make it, they say, "So-and-so is just an ordinary person just like me. So-and-so didn't finish school," or "This person had a child, but no matter what she went through, she finished school, and made it through. And if she can make it, so can I."

When you let people stop your dreams from coming true, you are giving them all the power. And you can't let people take any power from you.. Don't be afraid of losing a so-called friend because you are pursuing your goals and aspirations in life. No matter what stage of life you are in, people will always have something to say. They may say, "You think you're all that, now" or "You changed." So what? Yes you have changed, you have changed for the better. I think when you do go on a journey to do better for yourself, you will realize who was really for you and who wasn't and who's genuine. It's like a cleansing process. I always tell people there's a silver lining somewhere. It may hurt, but you get over it really quickly. Don't let that stop you. If you do, you will be living the shoulda, coulda, woulda life.

That's definitely something that you just want to keep in mind. I like to call it "In the dreams and formulations stage." You might have to keep those dreams to yourself, because again, everybody can't read blueprints, and when your dream is in that blueprint stage, don't expect everybody to see it as you do.

The Company You Keep

You want to make sure you're careful as to who you're surrounding yourself with on a daily basis. This goes back to the dream-killers. There may be some people that are just not ready to hear that dream, but you have so many people who are. You want to surround yourself with people who have like mindsets, people who are also pushing and trying to fulfill their dreams in life. You may need to get a mentor, someone who will help you through and give you that positive influence that's going to help you through certain situations.

I've had many friends in life (or so I liked to call them friends at one point), but at some point in time you realize they may have just been associates or they may have just been there for that period in your life. I believe that some people are there for just that portion of a timeframe, and some people are there for a lifetime.

You want to be careful with whom you're around, because sometimes you may have this dream or this purpose, and some people see that or realize that, and they purposefully try to keep you from realizing or going for your dream.

I had a, so called, friend who knew that I was working on some projects, and every time I turned around, he'd ask, "Did you see this show? Did you see that show?" I said, "No, I'm not watching TV right now. I'm really trying to bear down and work on my project." It became an issue where I wasn't giving him enough attention because I was giving too much attention to my dream. Needless to say, we're not friends anymore, but you win some and you lose some. I figure the friends who are supposed to be there, the family members who are supposed to be there, will be there.

Bad company can also come in the form of a family member. I can speak from experience. It's sad to say I have family members who have tried to tear me down. They would say, "Oh, she's always doing something. She's always selling something. She's always doing something good." You would think that would help them to change their mindset, but sometimes you can't change people. You can't change their mindset . . . And you shouldn't let it change you.

So many people struggle with saying 'no' to family. They spend a lifetime having their lives dictated by that whole family dynamic. It's very hard for people to break away from, no matter how much they try. It's almost like they're in a cult, and they just can't break away from the fact that no one has the right, whether blood or not, to do that to another human being. Don't ever let what a family member says reframe you; no matter if they're blood or they're not, no matter what, you definitely don't want to let the negative things and negativity of others, no matter who they are, bring you down.

The reality is we can't get rid of our family. I don't believe that just because you're related that gives anyone the right bring you down or anything else. But a lot of people have a really hard time with saying no or standing up for themselves when it comes to someone who's related to them, because a lot of families are built on that whole "blood is thicker than water; and you love your family no matter what they do; they can do no wrong. At the end of the day they're your family."

Yes, they may be your family, but they are not you. You are the person who has to live your life. You are the person who has to answer for you and to you.

You want to make sure that you're surrounding yourself with, and keeping yourself around, positive people who will in turn, help keep the positivity and creativity flowing. You may have to go to different meet-up groups and surround yourself with other like minded women. Go to events and seminars. Get yourself a mentor, someone who can help you through. Just surrounding yourself with those sorts of people can help your dream come into reality, just by that positive influence. Just being around that positivity helps your energy pick up, and it will help you to have a happier and more enthusiastic way of thinking.

In many cases, you may have to distance yourself. Love them from afar. That's what I've had to do. You can always love them, go to events, and call them, but get away quickly, if it starts to go into the negative, say, "Hey, I've got another call I've got to get on, but I love you and I'll talk to you later." Just don't let that negativity get you into a rut. You can still love somebody and keep it moving.

I can say this is a sad story or a heavy story. I've had some family members that, because of some of the things that I was doing, realize, "You have too much of the spotlight on you." And because they weren't doing anything positive, they tried to turn my positive into a negative. You never want to let that turn you around. Think about your end result. Where are you trying to go? What are your dreams? What is your purpose? Think about the lives that you will change, and make that be another stepping stone for where you're trying to go in life. You just might want to love them from afar. Say, "I love you, but I've got to go," and keep it pushing.

Obstacles

Obstacles are going to come. There are going to be trials, there are going to be tribulations, but you can't let that deter you. You may be in school. While raising my first son, I was in college. I had to work full-time, I had to go to school full-time, as well as be a mother. It got to the point where I thought, "I can't really afford school. I may have to drop out a little bit to pay the bills." But I figured some things out. Instead of just letting that deter me or let that be an obstacle, I found another way.

I researched. I found some grants. I found work-study. I made that obstacle into a stepping stone, something that would keep me going and something that would keep my dream going. Many times we hit that wall. We get in front of that brick wall, and it feels as if it's never going to be knocked down. Whatever you do, there's always something that comes and knocks you two or three steps back. But what you have to do is just regroup. Sometimes you may have to formulate another plan or set up a backup plan. But just don't let it stop you.

Because no matter what you do, no matter how famous you are or whatever the case, everybody has obstacles. Everybody has gone through something. If you come up to that roadblock or obstacle, just take a step, look at it, look at some options, make a plan, and figure out how you can keep going without stopping the dream, without stopping the purpose and push forward. You definitely don't want it to stop you. If you let that control you, then you'll never be able to push forward. In everything that you do, you want to believe and keep pushing. There are going to be hurdles and brick walls, but you've just got to break through them and jump over them.

I know some of you are saying that's easier said than done. Some of you may have to dig into a deeper space. All of us go through different trials and tribulations, some are more painful than others. There is a big thing often in the way called FEAR. I look at fear as Failure to Ever Achieving Reality. So many people are afraid of failing when trying to reach for those goals in life, when in reality, nothing's worst then having a dream and never going for it.

When we talk about things like going for a new career or trying to make extra money and things like that, I challenge people to look back on a time in their life when something so devastating happened that they did not think they would live through it. I think everyone has one of those moments in their life. I ask them to reflect on, "Remember that feeling?" Because I can remember those feelings and points in my life where it's "Oh, my God!" I see why people sometimes just want to check out. Everybody goes through that. That's just reality.

When we talk about moving towards our goals and dreams, so many people never do it because they're worried about failure or what other people will say, like people are going to laugh at them. "I told you so!" If you think about that moment when you overcame that thing you never thought you were going to be able to live through, and you compare it to trying something in life, there really is no comparison." If you survived that thing, whatever your thing is, why can't you step out and try a new career, try to make some extra money, whatever it may be?

And people say, "You know, that is so true. There was a moment in life that I was so devastated, something so horrible happened to me. And look, I'm still standing! So this really is nothing in comparison."

I want a deeper glimpse into your mindset when it comes to actually sitting there and saying, "I've been hit with this huge roadblock." Where do you go in your mind, and how? What is your process of getting past it so that you don't go off track, and you don't shrink back and give up?

For me the huge devastating road block that came and hit me like a ton of bricks was when my favorite person in the world, my grandmother, passed away. I had a business that was very, very lucrative. Not only was I making money, but I was helping other people to accumulate money and to live a happier and healthier life, and it just felt like everything was great. I was living the good life.

I remember my grandmother coming up to Philadelphia. She was visiting with us. She was only there for about seven days. I had a long day. I did a show, and when I came back, she wasn't feeling well and she said she was going to go lie down, so I went home. Before I fell asleep, I got a call from my mom stating that the ambulance was there and the paramedics were working on her. So I rushed back there only to find that my grandmother didn't make it.

That, right there, was the beginning of what I call my end. I felt like that was a moment that I was never going to get past. That was not only a brick wall, but it was a cement wall with something I couldn't push through. I didn't have that passion for my purpose any more. It was gone, because she was one of the people whom I wanted to see me fulfill my dreams.

But I've come to realize that even though that person couldn't be there to see or to push through, if that person was there, she would want to see me push through. She would want to see me succeed or excel. Do this, not only for you, but for the people around you and for the other people who need you. I just stopped doing what I was doing, but what about all the people who depended on me to help them get through to the next stage?

It took me a while to get through it. I prayed about it, and tried to keep myself in a positive mindset, even though it was extremely hard. Because, when you lose someone and you go through something that's so difficult, it's really hard. It's easier to say than to do, just bringing yourself back. But I started to think, "What would she want? What would she want to see me do?" And not only that, what about the people around me? If you're helping other people, they need to be lifted up by the things that you're doing.

In order to get past that, I suggest go into a deeper self and pray about it and realize that you can get through it. You're never going to get anywhere sitting in that same rut. When you wake up tomorrow, you'll be sitting in that same rut.

One of the things I've heard over the years is, "you don't have to be great to get started, but you have to get started to be great." You will never get anywhere just sitting around and letting the rut get deeper. It will only get worse. It may take day after day, or a day at a time, but you want to keep pushing. It's better to get up. Everybody's going to fall and everybody's going to hit that wall, but once you get up and start to make that effort, even if it's hard, each day will get better with time.

The Day You Stop Making Excuses

"Excuses, excuses, excuses," is what I like to call them. I did a survey on hundreds of women asking the question, "What is keeping you from your dreams? What is keeping you from your purpose? What is keeping you from fulfilling the things that you want in life?" I got so many answers, and 95% of the answers were all excuses. "I have kids, I'm a mother," or "I didn't finish school," or "I have a family member to take care of," or "Everybody's dependent upon me." The number one answer that just really got under my skin was, "I don't have time."

"I don't have time" was the number one thing that people said was keeping them from pursuing their dreams. I thought it would be fear. I thought fear would be the number one excuse that kept people from getting to their dreams accomplished. I don't know if they're making excuses because of fear, which could be possible, yet so many people are making excuses because they don't want to get something done. I've done it myself in terms of success. If I think something is not going to work out, I say, "I'll just wait until I'm prepared." I've definitely been that person who has pushed things off because of fear of it not going right. But I had to get out of that mind-set. I had to stop making excuses and just do it. You just have to get out of that mindset, because otherwise you'll never get it done, and keep making excuses.

If time is the issue, you have to sit down and think, "How am I spending my time?" Many people are on social media all day or they're watching TV. If you just start to take an inventory of your time in 15-minute increments, trust me, it will change your life. Just take your day and break it down by 15-minute increments, and you'll see how much time is wasted talking on the phone, gossiping, or whatever the latest show would be. If you just took that time and started putting in slots in terms of getting some motivation, reading a book, or going to a seminar. Start adding in positive things (planning and goal-setting). It will definitely change, not only your mindset, but it will change your whole way of thinking in terms of "I don't have enough time." Many of these excuses are keeping us from our ultimate goal. Just look at some of the things that are keeping you from doing what you're meant to do or what you're supposed to do, based on an excuse.

We all have that ability to say, "I'll go tomorrow," or, "It's raining, I don't feel like going." Those are all excuses. Once you start breaking down that barrier of making excuses, you'll be able to get more done, and you'll be able to start realizing that you do have time and you can fulfill your purpose.

That's so important. When you talk about surrounding yourself with certain people, I have found that being around people who are so much further ahead of me - and we all have people who are further ahead (everything is relative). When you're around people like that and people who just have this higher level, you find yourself striving more. In order to get to another level in life you must be willing to do the things the average person will not do, and that requires, maybe, working on holidays. Everyone says, "Oh, my Goodness, it's a holiday!" Well, in my world, my people are all working on holidays. They don't even know it's a holiday half the time. They're like, "Oh, it's Christmas? I didn't even realize it's Christmas!" Some people frown upon that, but those are the little things, that, it honestly takes to get ahead in life and to build on something where you never have to worry about working on a Christmas or working ever again. Sometimes it's sacrifice so that down the road you never have to even lift a finger.

Often people use excuses and reasons why they are not going to do something. "I'm not doing all that. It's a holiday, or it's this and it's that." You have to change your mindset. You have to think in the mind of a champion. I was talking to my mentor, Vicki Irvin, when writing this book and she talked about how she works out in a gym with professional athletes. People with a success mindset are so far ahead of the average everyday person. And just being around this type of person can help to push you to the next level as well. As long as I have people whom I'm like, it will help to keep me on my toes. It helps me to have an even stronger mindset. So I stay surrounded by people who are working towards the highest level of everything they do. There's a highest level of everything in life, and I love to surround myself with people who are like that.

I look at and study some of the most successful people and their philosophies, the majority of them were not handed success, nor was it inherited. Most started from the bottom, dead-broke, homeless, government housing. They did not know how they were going to make it. A lot of times when we see successful people, we like to try to discredit them and say they inherited it or had it handed to them. These are people I like to go to dinner with and hang with and hear how they speak and talk and what they do to push themselves through, and that pushes me. When I'm tired and I talk to somebody like that, I think, "What would so-and-so do? What would so-and-so say?" I think that's so important that we don't make excuses and part of that is making sure we're not in the company of people who do make excuses for a living.

We all have two sets of friends. When something is going right in our life, we have the friend we can call and we know they're going to side with us no matter what we say. "Yes, girl, yes! I understand."

Then we have the people we know that if we call them and we give them the story, they're going to be like, "You know you're wrong. You know you need to do this."

In life, you have to make a choice. Who's really going to help push you to the next level? Is it the yes-men or is the people who are going to tell you the truth? So it's important that we stay around people who don't allow those excuses because they don't live their lives like that, and we wouldn't dare open up our mouth around them, making those types of excuses. I think that's really important.

Your Purpose

Many people struggle with purpose. This goes all across the board, but when you're younger, at least for me, you don't even think about those things. You're just out there. You're trying to go to college and get a job or whatever, you don't even think about purpose. I think that's a natural progression when we get older in life and we have more responsibility. We start thinking about, "What am I doing every day? I'm going to a job that I really don't like," or, "I'm living a life that's not really me, and I feel like I was destined to do something greater and be used in a different way."

So that epiphany hits people at all different points in time, but typically it doesn't happen until you're older. A few people are fortunate enough to understand early on, that they had a purpose. I know if you said something to me about purpose in my twenties, I would have been like, "What are you talking about?" When you get older, you start getting a little bit more profound and introspective, and you start thinking on a deeper level, and you realize that there's more to life than just being all about me. This happens for people at so many different points in time.

I truly believe everybody was born and sent here for a purpose, whether it be your purpose to be a mother or a caregiver or a teacher or a millionaire, whatever it may be. Everyone has a purpose, no matter what it is. I look at my mother. She's always had that caring aspect, and everybody just loves her, they want to go to her house. She's, "Are you hungry? You want something to eat?" She's always had that personality to care for people, so she started a daycare and the kids absolutely love her. The parents love sending their kids there. When it's time for the kids to leave, they don't want to leave. That's her purpose. That's what she was sent here to do: to be a caregiver, to take care of people.

Your purpose could be that of a caregiver or a teacher. Some people have a gift of teaching. They may be good with teaching people how to learn in different ways. You have people who are gifted at singing, or dancing or drawing. It was something you were born with or have a passion to do. It's something that can't be taken away from you. Some people know their purpose early on in life or some people realize it later in life. I believe when you start chasing your dream you will run into your purpose, doing whatever it is you were meant to do.

I didn't always know my purpose. There were many years, when I said this is it. This is what I'm supposed to be doing. But not too long after that I didn't feel fulfilled. It took a lot of searching. I actually didn't realize that when I once lost my passion for helping people that that was actually my purpose. It took losing it, to realize what it was. When I started back into the business of helping people, several years later, that's when I said I will never let it go again. I didn't realize how many people I was letting down, because I was being selfish and keeping my purpose all to myself. I get excited when I help people bring change to their lives. It's my purpose and it's what makes me happy doing what I do. If you get an email from one person you were able to help save their house, or help them keep their children in private school, or help them take care of their elderly parents and be able to buy the medicine their parents can't afford, that's life-changing to these people and that's real purpose.

I think sometimes a lot of people get confused, and we think that to really impact the world or life, we have to do it on a large scale, like an Oprah Winfrey, when few of us will ever be to that level. That's just the odds and how life works out. As long as it matters most to you, it's all that matters.

Your purpose should never be compared or measured up to anyone else's. You have the Oprahs, but then you have the everyday people like you and me. Every once in a while I may get an e-mail from someone thanking me for the extra money that I showed they could bring into their household, which is life-changing to people. Everything is relative. It doesn't have to be about a million dollars or this or that. An extra $500 a month can keep a person in their house the rest of their life, and that's life-changing to that person. That's all that matters.

You shouldn't get confused thinking that it has to be on this grand scale where we have these huge platforms on TV and we can touch millions of lives. That's going to be few and far between. But if you can help one person little by little, that's living purpose, and that's really important.

The Plan

Many people are looking to be successful in life, but they're running through without a plan, without any set rules in terms of how they're going to get there. "What do I need to do in order to be successful? What do I need to do in order to fulfill my purpose?"

As we mentioned earlier, just changing one person's life can be a major difference, but what are you going to do to help change that one life? Have you set those ground rules? What is step one? What is step two? Take a minute to sit down and write down the goals and what it takes to get there, to plan it out and plan the way that it will work; the way that it should work.

Even if you need to have a Plan B and C, you need to do that. Just sit down and get the whole thing planned out. Without a plan, you can be all over the place. For instance, "I'm going to make this certain amount of money." Okay, but how? How are you going to do that, and what is your goal per day? What is your goal per week? You might have a grand scheme or goal of "I want to earn $100,000 a year." What does it take to do that? If you break that down into small increments, it makes it more realistic. It makes it better in terms of "I've reached this part of my goal. Now what's next?" If you sit down and have a plan as to how you're going to get there and how you're going to achieve that goal, then it makes it so much easier and worthwhile.

One of the things that I think is really cliché with people is planning and goal-setting. We hear people say, "Set the goals and have a business plan and do this." People want to skip all these steps because we live in a world where it's all about instant gratification. Having a plan in your head is very different from having a plan that you've written out and you look at every day and you check off the points that you've covered already. When you keep stuff in your head, that's subject to all types of craziness that can actually go on. Even though writing down goals sounds like a cliché, it really makes a difference. I'm speaking from experience.

When I try to keep things in my head, I think "This isn't working." But when I put things in black and white, and I have something to look at, and a checkpoint and something to check off, I know where I'm at. I know if I'm progressing, I know if I'm BS-ing, basically.

Have a plan of execution. I'm not saying that it has to be carved in stone, because everything is subject to change. We think things are going to go one way, but at the end of the day, we can't control life and obstacles, and we have to re-route a lot. But having a basic framework for a plan is going to be very, very important in life. It's definitely a step that you cannot skip.

Implementation

Implementation is something that people overlook all the time. As we talked about goal-setting and planning, people can plan and goal-set all day, but without implementation of these goals and these plans, they won't get anywhere.

I can tell you from my own experiences, where I had journals and books with plans – everything written down to the T – but without implementation these goals and plans, were just some handwriting in a book. It won't be something that is being worked upon or a goal that's being reached.

Years ago I used to say, "Okay, let me just write down a couple things and stick it on my mirror, or write a couple of things and put it where I can see it. This way I know I'm working towards that." Yeah, you see it, but if you're not actually creating any action towards those goals or plans, then nothing is going to happen.

I know sometimes people will buy a bunch of home study courses. I love to learn and I love to read. I'm always reading and researching and getting the home study courses. But again, without that implementation, you won't get anywhere. You have to sit down and not only go over your goals, but start writing down when each goal should be completed. Start implementing those goals and set aside the time to have everything finished.

Some people get, what we call accountability partners, where that person can help to push you along and say, "Did you get this thing done yet? Did you get that thing done yet?" Sometimes it takes me to have that accountability partner or coach or mentor to push me along and say, "How is this going? Have you started that yet?" In many cases, you may have people who don't have that accountability partner. And if you don't, it's okay. It won't stop you or deter you from what you're trying to do in life. You'll just have to set some timers.

Before you can move onto Goal #2, Goal #1 has to be accomplished, Plan #1 has to be accomplished. You have to sit down and make sure that everything that you have for that Step 1 is done before you move onto Step 2. That's a major requirement with fulfilling and being successful within your purpose: making sure you're implementing the things that will get you to the next level.

I see a lot of people who are into self-investment, and they'll invest in a seminar or a course. They'll get all of this knowledge, but at the end of the day, when they go home, what are they going to do with the information that they learned? Are they going to put it into action? Are they going to take the steps needed to make it actually work or are they going to stick it on the shelf? I have a mentor who says, "There's self-help and then there's shelf-help," where you just stick it on the shelf. Where are you going to be in life when you're doing that?

There are people who convince themselves that they're working on themselves and their business by attending seminars, but at the end of the day all they're doing is being a seminar junkie. You can go to all the seminars you want. You can gain, you can talk the talk and do everything, but if you're not implementing what you learn, you're really not moving forward. When you get back in the space by yourself, and you have to discipline yourself and dedicate time and attention to moving forward, it's difficult for a lot of people, which is why it's important for people to attach to mentors.

At the highest level, everyone has somebody else pushing them. It's so hard to do. Self-motivation is very limited. We all have different levels of it, and some of us may be more self-motivated than others, but we all hit a wall where we need somebody else to push us over.

That's why when you talking about the implementation step, there's also a piece of making sure you invest in the most important asset, which is yourself, and you make sure you attach to mentors and accountability partners and people who are going to hold you accountable to actually taking the action and implementing; otherwise it doesn't get you very far. You can have all the knowledge you want, you can have all the skill that you want, and you can know every step you're supposed to do, but if you don't put it into action, it means nothing. It's really, really important to implement.

Reinvent Yourself

Now, that you have started the process of your purpose and your great success, it's now time that you sit down and think about the different things you may have to change or certain facets in your life that may have to realign themselves with your success; now it's time to reinvent.

Now that you maybe have that right circle of people who you need to be around to change your mindset or to help you grow and challenge you in life, you've sat down and gone over your time schedule, and you've gone over your plan and you've set your goals, now it's time for the reinvention. Now it's time for you to prepare for your success.

Have you ever changed your hairstyle, hair color, outfit or made any type of change and someone said, there is something different about you, but I don't know what it is. Those are the type of responses you will get when you start to reinvent the new you. People will notice that something has been changed, but they will not be able to put their finger on it. They will be more attracted to you. You will have a new confidence, a new swag, a new way of looking at things in life. And trust me, people will notice.

Get ready for the new you. Once you have started to implement your dreams, started to believe in yourself, have gotten rid of toxic people in your life, gotten past those obstacles, stopped making excuses, planned and implemented those plans, people will notice that you mean business. They will start to see you are a take charge, get it done, type of person who they want to attach themselves to.

Of course you will have those naysayers, and haters, that say you have changed. You can proudly say, "Thank you. Yes, I have." There is nothing wrong with change, as long as it's change for the better.

Some people say, "This was the old me." You want to be ready for this new you, for this new success that will follow you. Because once you start to implement the plan that you set, you'll definitely start to see the change.

Remember to align yourself with positive people who only want to see the best for you. The negative people will only try to pull you down. Make it a habit to think positive thoughts and not allow negative talk around you. Negativity only plants seeds, that starts to germinate in your mind.

Make your reinvention a celebration. However you like to celebrate; with friends, family, a night on the town, prayer, church, a get together, ice-cream and cake, however you like to to it, make it a grand occasion. Say goodbye to the old you, and get prepared for the reinvention of you. You deserve it.

Get Ready to Win, and Expect to Win!

Now that you've been working on your dream and purpose you will start to see change and transition. You want to make sure you are prepared for what comes next "SUCCESS!" One of my favorite motivational speakers I love to listen to, is Mr. Zig Ziglar. He says, "You were born to win, but in order to be the winner you were meant to be, you must plan to win, prepare to win, and expect to win." Just think about it, what happens to the majority of people who win the the lottery or come into a lot of money? They usually go bankrupt within the first year or two. Why? Because they are not prepared and they were not ready to manage that kind of money.

You don't want to get ready when success hits you, you want to be ready! When people are not ready to win or expecting to win, and success hit them, they are pulled in all directions without a plan in place. You can easily go over budget trying to put things in place at the last minute. For instance, if you're starting a business or getting ready to be successful, start looking into obtaining an accountant, or start looking into getting a lawyer who will help you with your business plan as you start to get your business formulated. You want to start preparing financially; get a financial advisor. Some people may come into certain terms of success so quickly that they weren't ready for it. Even if you have a business and you don't have your website up, or your website is up and you just weren't expecting 150 people to go onto your site and it crashes your site, expect to win, and be prepared to win. You don't want to have to get ready. You want to be ready.

You never know, you could be introduced to someone or asked, at a moments notice, to produce your business plan, or asked to showcase your talents at a major event, if you're not ready, you could miss that grand opportunity. Always have your elevator pitch ready. My mentor, Vicki Irvin, always states to always that you should be able to define who you are and what you do, without confusing the person. So practice your elevator pitch. Know what you have to offer people.

Have faith, believe in yourself, follow your plan and make sure every detail is implemented, and you will see success. Be ready.

Your Triumph

We're all pushing towards victory, whatever victory is. From person to person, it's very subjective and very different. Everybody goes through something in life. It's a part of your story, a part of your success. I will never, ever forget; I was at a seminar, and Les Brown was speaking. I was in awe of his story and the way that he told it. He had captured everybody's attention. I was hanging on every word. He was saying, "You need to be able to tell people who you are. You have to have a story."

I was thinking, "Man, I don't have a story. I didn't go through anything enough to actually have a story to tell." I hadn't been anywhere. But when you think about it, a lot of the obstacles that you've been through, a lot of the brick walls that I talked about earlier, are things you've overcome. Even down to your fear, down to the excuses, all of these are obstacles that you've overcome to bask in your glory and your triumph.

Don't be afraid of the things that happened in your past. People say, "I have scars." Be proud of your scars. Your testimony could change many people's lives. People who hear your testimony, about what happened to you, or who see what you went through and witness your end result will make them think, "Wow, she went through that, and here she is. She's still standing." That triumph can help so many other people. Never, ever be afraid of your story. Embrace it. Embrace who you are, and what you went through. Embrace where you're going, and confidence will definitely follow you. It will make you shine even brighter at the end of the day.

Don't wait until you get to your ultimate goal; celebrate along the way. I think sometimes we don't celebrate the small steps and the small achievements as we head towards the ultimate goal, and I think we need to do that. The journey is not easy, so it is important to give yourself credit.

We see people when they've made it, especially when we're looking at them from afar; it's almost like a fantasy Land. "They've made it. They look so great. But it's not an overnight success. There was just nobody paying them any attention or following them around with cameras when they were living out of their car or eating beans out of a can. We don't see that, so we get a very misconstrued idea of what success is about.

The reality is it's a long road of failure and setbacks, but the strong survive. The people who believe in themselves and their vision survive. I think it's important for people to resist becoming jaded by thinking individuals just randomly jump on the scene and make it, because it's not true. There's a journey and there's a process.

During your personal journey you may tend to look at someone else's end result and say, "Wow! They have 100 thousand followers on social media." Or "Wow, look at all the fabulous pictures and video's they are posting with fast cars, beautiful homes, money, vacation, and the perfect life." Stop it right there! Some people are what we call social media famous, but in reality it may not be the truth. Or you just may not have seen all they have been through to get to that point. You have to learn to stay in your own lane.

There are so many people looking for society's approval. You don't need anyone's consent in terms of who you are and what you want to be in this life. People may be on Facebook and just waiting for validation to get this many likes or that many likes. In reality, that's not what the overall goal is. A lot of people may look at your posts or may look at your life, and they never say anything.

Some people will say, "You've been such an inspiration to me just by who you are and the things that you say," and you never even know who's looking at you. You never know who's looking at you from afar when you're not even thinking about it. The things that you do in life, or the people that you help, you never know who's looking. Always strive to be your best even when no one's looking and you won't even realize how many lives you will begin to change.

I had a young lady tell me, "You've been such an inspiration. I've been watching you from afar, and something just drew me to you." I hadn't even realized that just the little things that you do in life will help somebody in so many different ways.

You don't have to be validated by what other people say, or how many clicks or likes that you get, just know that in your heart you're truly doing the right thing, and you're going after your dream in your own way. Trust me, once you get there, each step of the way you can look back and say, "Wow, I've made it up another step. I've climbed another step. I've reached another corner, another valley." Those are the things that will validate you. You validate your own self. You don't have to worry about other people or what they say. As long as you know that in your heart you're doing what's right for you and what you love to do, that's all that matters.

Your victory is yours, your triumph is a part of what makes you unique and what makes you, you. At the end of the day when you have reached all your goals, conquered all your fears, stopped making all the excuses, and taken on a whole new you, you will be able to look back and say I am Living my Life on Purpose with No Excuses!!!

About The Author

Yolanda was born and raised in West Philadelphia. She currently resides in the Carolina's, with her two boys Nameer and Quadeir. Yolanda encourages everyone to chase their dreams no matter how big they are. Find a way, make a way to Live Your Life On Purpose, No Excuses.

Keep up with Yolanda McCutcheon on her page. ***www.YolandaMcCutcheon.com***, *and on social media.*